Kernels for Growth — Sprinkle with Love

Journal for Self-Reflection
and Poetry to Stir Your Soul

by

Nathalie M. Léger

"Delight in the discoveries and
the precious moments along the way."

CCB Publishing
British Columbia, Canada

Kernels for Growth – Sprinkle with Love:
Journal for Self-Reflection and Poetry to Stir Your Soul

Copyright ©2021 by Nathalie M. Léger
ISBN-13   978-1-77143-491-1
First Edition

Library and Archives Canada Cataloguing in Publication
Title: Kernels for growth – sprinkle with love : journal for self-reflection
and poetry to stir your soul / by Nathalie M. Léger.
Other titles: Sprinkle with love
Names: Léger, Nathalie M., author
Description: First edition. | "Delight in the discoveries and the precious
moments along the way."
Identifiers: Canadiana 2021022486X | ISBN 9781771434911 (softcover)
Subjects: LCSH: Self-actualization (Psychology)—Problems, exercises, etc.
| LCSH: Self-actualization (Psychology)—Poetry. | LCSH: Diaries—Authorship.
Classification: LCC BF637.S4 L44 2021 | DDC 158.1—dc23

All poems and essays contained herein are copyright Nathalie M. Léger.

Cover artwork credit: © Nathalie M. Léger

Extreme care has been taken by the author to ensure that all information presented in this book is accurate and up to date at the time of publishing. Neither the author nor the publisher can be held responsible for any errors or omissions. Additionally, neither is any liability assumed for damages resulting from the use of the information contained herein.

All rights reserved. No part of this publication may be reproduced, stored in a retrieval system or transmitted in any form or by any means, electronic, mechanical, photocopying, recording or otherwise without the express written permission of the publisher, except by a reviewer who may quote brief passages in a review.

Publisher: CCB Publishing
             British Columbia, Canada
             www.ccbpublishing.com

To my Beloved Grandmother

Your guidance is a treasure
wrapped in heavenly love.

Contents

Acknowledgements ix
Preface xi
Introduction xiii
Poetry – Oneness 1
Poetry – Wings of Remembrance 2
Soulful Imagery – Being Enough 3
Kernels for Growth:
#1 Embracing Your Calling 5
#2 Rising to Freedom 7
#3 Purity of Your Heart 9
#4 Dwelling in Gratitude 11
#5 Dreams in Discovery 13

Poetry – Divine Connection 15
Poetry – Just be YOU 16
Soulful Imagery – Timeless Beauty 17
Kernels for Growth:
#6 Dancing with Life 19
#7 Bold Celebration 21
#8 True Surrender 23
#9 Communicating with Love 25
#10 Seeking Adventure 27

Poetry – Imagination 29
Poetry – Dreams in Flight 30
Soulful Imagery – In Awe of the Moment 31
Kernels for Growth:
#11 Aware in Wonder 33
#12 Simplicity of the Moment 35
#13 Fear Less 37
#14 Inclusive Collaboration 39
#15 Act of Love 41

Poetry – In Sync 43
Poetry – Magic of the Heart 44
Soulful Imagery – Everyday Magic 45
Kernels for Growth:
#16 Inner Beauty 47
#17 Purposeful Goodness 49
#18 Making Time 51
#19 Romance is in the Air 53
#20 Developing Intuition 55

Poetry – Timing of a Moment 57
Poetry – If You Know Love, Then You Do 58
Soulful Imagery – Divine Feminine 59
Kernels for Growth:
#21 Silent Vows 61
#22 Ernest Accountability 63
#23 Endless Generosity 65
#24 Honouring Creativity 67
#25 Joyful Introspection 69

Poetry – Inward Vows 71
Poetry – Mirror of Enchantment 72
Soulful Imagery – A New Dawn 73
Kernels for Growth:
#26 Enabling Truth 75
#27 Leading with Courage 77
#28 Success in Layers 79
#29 Finding Peace 81
#30 Desire to Prosper 83

Poetry – Rewarding Pause 85
Poetry – On a Journey to Love 86
Soulful Imagery – The Lover's Journey 87

Epilogue 89
Your Journal 91

Acknowledgements

I blew a kiss to the sky above
One faithful wish to my star of love
I knelt and bowed to the earth
Nurtured by nature's love since birth
I had a vision of an eagle in flight
It flew proudly into the night
I drew a heart around the moon
While envisioning a
Thousand petals in bloom.

I wrote this poem and named it **Star Seed Dreams**. It reminds me of how we are constantly planting seeds and working towards the manifestation of our dreams. We can spend countless hours pondering and patiently waiting for those seeds to bloom into life. As I sit here and prepare this acknowledgement, I am struck by the realization that I am in the here and now writing my very first book for publication. It is exciting, yet surreal. I am watching the seeds that I have sown sprout before my very eyes.

I want to take this moment to share how grateful I am for the support and encouragement I have received from my family and friends. I am honoured to spend these cherished moments with you, and you have been such an inspiration and an integral part of this journey. You have always encouraged me to celebrate and grow from this beloved passion that I have for writing. You envisioned a book in the horizon even before I did. Your love, your enthusiasm and your collaboration have been invaluable. I want to offer my sincere gratitude to my dear friends who have helped me revise and refine my creative musings. I appreciate the generous amount of time you have spent reading my poetry and the numerous hours we have spent brainstorming and sharing in deep conversations. You have all brought your distinctive blend of talents and energy to this venture. I love and treasure every one of you. I am so grateful, and I am so proud to be walking alongside you throughout this most endearing adventure.

I want to thank Paul Rabinovitch at CCB Publishing for offering me this great opportunity and helping me put together in print and in production this gift that I will treasure. Your insights, your time and your authenticity are genuinely appreciated.

May you all enjoy this great dance with life and connect to the flame inside your heart that burns brightly. May all your seeds of manifestation bloom into your most cherished dreams come true.

The best is yet to come!

Preface

> She melded with the quiet
> And listened to the musings
> From within.
> She was immersed in the
> Hum that swayed her, an
> Invitation from the energy
> Dancing in her belly.
> She was moved by the
> Rhythm of her harmonious
> Breath, in sync with
> Every beat of her loving heart.

I named this poem **In the Quiet**. It describes how I feel when I am writing. I share this beautiful dance with words and ride on the waves of inspiration. I connect with this flowing energy that is filled with so much love and peace. I am aware that I am part of this exhilarating experience that we call Life, and there are so many layers to uncover on this extraordinary journey.

I am celebrating five decades of explorations, experiences and lessons that have been gifted to me by so many incredible teachers. I appreciate that every step along the way has been essential, and that every person I have met has been incredibly valuable in helping me discover the tools I needed for my personal development. I value that learning is a never-ending journey, and that I am always in the process of harvesting new nuggets of insight. I have always possessed a deep curiosity and fascination with human behaviour, but I also share a great love and interest in the workings of the Universe. My preference has always been to follow my intuition as I have learned that my life flows with greater ease when I do not get caught up in all the thoughts that are running through my mind. I believe that we all have a unique way of communing with something much greater than ourselves, beyond the scope of understanding it completely. I trust that we are guided towards our highest good and purpose, when we are actively participating and co-creating with the opportunities that are presented to us. When we intentionally want to co-create with the unseen, we raise our awareness to be more in tune with the signs, following the arrows and connecting the dots. I believe that we create our reality, and that life can truly feel magical when we allow our story to unfold from the passion in our hearts.

I have been a witness to this intriguing adventure for some time now. I derive a lot of amusement and fulfillment in co-creating with a love that I have come to know as my confidant, sidekick, mentor, protector, and muse – this multidimensional universe. I am devoted to the guidance and the teachings, and I am always interested in discovering more. I have found my passion and true love in the beating of my own heart. My wish for you is that you have found or will find your true love in the beating of your very own.

If you have any questions or would like to share your thoughts or share your stories, you can connect with me by email at the following address: **kernelsforgrowth@hotmail.com**

With Love,
Nathalie

Introduction

We all have an individual purpose. Every twist and turn on our path is meant to wake us up to the truth and meaning of our lives. Are we not more than just this physical shell in which we make our way in the world? Yes, this is the vehicle that was meant to carry us through the journey, but are we not more?

As you slowly peel back the layers and reveal little by little who you are, every dream that has been hiding behind the shelf, lost beneath a pile of other commitments and responsibilities, will come flooding back to you. It is in that moment of recollection that you will remember how it feels to be truly alive. This journal is meant to inspire you and invite you to connect to those shining moments in your life that light you up. It is also an invitation to seek out and discover hidden truths and desires. Every kernel you uncover is a gemstone for growth. When sprinkled with love, you are inviting miracles to occur throughout your days. Your journey can be a truly uplifting adventure. I am honoured to share this time with you. So now, let's have fun!

There are 30 kernels of experience I have found enriching on my personal growth journey and I have introduced each by:

- a contemplation
- a personal mantra
- a reflection posed as a question that you can journal about
- a power word that you can meditate on
- a quote to support and deepen your meditative exploration.

I have also included soulful imagery and poetry inspired by events and experiences I have encountered on my path. Many of these were inspired by the amazing people I have met along the way who opened my heart in unimaginable ways. Writing has always been a passion of mine, but through the years it has developed in new and fascinating ways. My union with writing goes beyond anything I could have ever dreamed would come true. It is one that takes me on these voyages of pure emotional bliss. It is a safe place for me to dwell and fall in love, with these invitations to surrender and connect with my inner muse who is eager to come out and play. It is a marriage of ultimate peace and a commitment that succeeds in making my creative heart soar with enchantment. I am grateful for these moments of inspiration and I am always quite surprised at what flows through me and wishes to be revealed.

Oneness

We are here together enmeshed in the fabric of this universe and each of us impacts one another in a myriad of ways. Whether we are of the same family or complete strangers, we are made of the same stars and beautiful essence of creation. We have been birthed into this world to illuminate it with radiance and offer our innate gifts, which help humanity to grow and prosper in all forms.

Wings of Remembrance

You were not born to be mediocre;
you were designed to be magnificent
and stay true to your light.

You may have been conditioned
to follow a crowd,
yet the very breath from
which you came
is still the truest part of you.

Although you may not always
remember, sometimes you
are meant to forget.

The journey is revealed
step by step,
so spread your wings
with no regrets.

Nathalie M. Léger

Soulful Imagery – Being Enough

I smile at the gold I find within my heart. I collect every nugget with care and I am grateful for the generous insights they bear. The seeds of wisdom bloom in groves and the sparkling gems illuminate my steps. The breaths of freedom offer my dreams…emergence. These are the precious gifts that Life presents, shining in moments laced with kisses and blessings of Heaven's love.

I walk a path of adventure and give myself permission to be tempted by the Unknown. I love the idea of this grand mystery that may at times leave me perplexed, yet curious and eager to explore. I am seduced by this feeling of undying devotion to this great orchestra in the sky. I live in a world of fanciful strings, and I am awake to this breathtaking splendour in being alive.

I dive into the depths of knowledge and uncover new ways of merging with Life. I am at one with this flame that lives at the core of my being. It is ignited by the glimpses of inner and outer worlds. I find myself deeply submerged in this mystical creation; it is unfolding through the fortitude and light to which I pray. There is no room for doubt as this transformation reveals the ingenuity of every moment.

I live a life that is fueled by inspiration as I witness the capricious intricacies that make their way into my day. I am both amused and fascinated by the workings of this web that is woven so perfectly in the fabric of the universe. I am one small speck in this ocean of life, yet my being is important, as I add to the magnificent tapestry of this world's wonder.

I seek to draw out and entertain every seedling of creativity, and I am riveted by the way they choose to reveal themselves. I am merely the instrument through which these sentiments are finding expression. I find myself touched by the emotions in which I find my heart being romanced, both from the energy and the visions they conjure. I am grateful for this beautiful gift that I am passionately committed to… explore.

I sit in a field of creation and I invite my heart to speak. I listen actively to every word and partake with an open mind in this most endearing and harmonious conversation. I am lifted and renewed by this invigorating clarity. I take the steps necessary to move forward and find myself growing from this space, fully engrossed and aware of the magic that is taking place.

I have been a witness to each moment of success and each moment of disappointment. They have sat in silence and in celebration of one another, forging an alliance in which both have acquired the understanding that they are mutually inclusive and beneficial in helping me to grow in confidence and resilience.

I grow from this everlasting energy that inspires me to learn and master my craft. I am in tune with the resurgence of ideas and the awakened fiery love that lives to create. I am immersed in a field of dreams and floating through incarnations, filled with memories that beckon me to write about my journey on the path to which I was born to awaken.

I am the narrator in my story. I am deeply intertwined with this bountiful essence of creation that supports me in designing a life that I value in which I thrive. I am worthy of unconditional love and from this innate belief, I therefore live a life of simply Being Enough.

#1 - Embracing Your Calling

Your calling is your signature card; it is unique and yours alone. When you listen to the whispers of your soul, you fly on the wings of purpose that carry you off to greet the wondrous meaning of your existence. There is no other person in this world that can take your place; it has been reserved for you to make your life absolutely...**Awesome**!

Personal Mantra:

I am listening to the call of my heart and I do not turn away from what I know and feel to be true.

Personal Reflection:

If you were to describe the vision you have for your life in a few lines or in a brief paragraph, what would it be?

_____

_____

_____

_____

_____

_____

_____

_____

_____

Power Word:

Purpose

> **"Your PURPOSE can be discovered through the hobbies that inspire you."**

#2 - Rising to Freedom

You are the magician in your own life. You can honour your passions by following your heart's yearnings. You can rise freely by simply diving into those special moments that light you up. You can hold the wand and cast your most beautiful…**Spell!**

Personal Mantra:

I am en route to discovering the treasures of my inner world that give rise to my personal best.

Personal Reflection:

What activity gives you the most exhilarating feeling of aliveness?

_____
_____
_____
_____
_____
_____
_____
_____
_____
_____
_____
_____

Kernels for Growth – Sprinkle with Love

Power Word:

Passion

> **"Your PASSION is the rocket fuel that accelerates the lift you need to succeed."**

#3 - Purity of Your Heart

There comes a time in each of our lives when someone sees something so beautiful in us that they offer a reflection, magnifying the treasure we truly are. They celebrate our victories and the choices we make with so much support and encouragement. They do not let us waiver in fear and doubt. This person does not come around every day, but you know when they show up because you feel their heart and their love without questioning their intentions. Their spirit is pure and the energy they exude is a shower of divine…**Bliss**!

Personal Mantra:

I am open to receive the support of someone who has my best interest at heart.

Personal Reflection:

Can you recall a time when you met such a person and how did it change your life?

_____
_____
_____
_____
_____
_____
_____
_____

Kernels for Growth – Sprinkle with Love

Power Word:

Kindness

"The sweetness in KINDNESS is one to be savoured."

#4 - Dwelling in Gratitude

Every morning is a new beginning. Practising gratitude not only aligns you with the flow of life, it also creates a space where you feel the genuine empowerment of confidence and the sheer joy of being... **Alive!**

Personal Mantra:

I am grateful to wake up every morning feeling excited about the wonderful new adventures that await my daring willingness to engage in life.

Personal Reflection:

What did you wake up feeling grateful for this morning?

_____
_____
_____
_____
_____
_____
_____
_____
_____
_____
_____
_____

Kernels for Growth – Sprinkle with Love

Power Word:

Appreciation

"APPRECIATION is the joy that further enhances your awareness of the experience."

#5 - Dreams in Discovery

Happiness is found in your inner garden, not in someone else's. You cannot search in another's pocket to find your dreams. The meaning of your life starts with you, when you discover your inner voice, and you use it to master your outer life in service and...**Purpose!**

Personal Mantra:

I am diving into the well of my inner being and coming up with jewels that inspire a life that radiates generosity and kindness.

Personal Reflection:

If you had no time or money concerns, how would you envision yourself to be of service to others?

_____
_____
_____
_____
_____
_____
_____
_____
_____
_____
_____

Kernels for Growth – Sprinkle with Love

Power Word:

Intention

> **"The degree of clarity that you bring to your INTENTION will enrich the outcome."**

Nathalie M. Léger

Divine Connection

A ray of sunlight
pierces through
a cloudy sky.

I bathe in the
warmth of light
that twinkles
on my face.

I love the
gentle tug
I feel
in my heart.

I envision
this golden thread
of glitter
that connects
me to the infinite
glow of the
Universe.

Just be YOU

The true nature
of your emotions
floats in the
ocean of your heart.

There is a current
that you align with
when you follow
your soul's compass.

The world you see
is found within
and the sea you
travel is up to you.

Once you skipper
your ebbs and
flows, you will
find yourself
navigating to every
destination that
you were ever
meant to go.

Just be YOU - Complete!

Nathalie M. Léger

Soulful Imagery – Timeless Beauty

The light shone down and illuminated her face. A smile grew in her eyes where tears once relentlessly shared a home. She knelt and gazed at the wide-open sky. Layers of blue and white cotton, a masterpiece of love. There was no cost to feeling this warmth that was so lovingly blanketing her soul. The radiance of this omnipresent affection was without price. It was absolute and it was pure. A force far greater than any other, to see just in that moment. She bowed and kissed the earth, feeling within her, peace with All.

She wandered in the lush forest, admiring the colours of the autumn leaves and the sound of them crunching under her feet. She took in long breaths of fresh air and scented pine, which invigorated her senses. All the world's madness slipped away in that moment. It was nice to get away, lost in the neighbouring woodlands, finding refuge and a sense of normalcy that seemed to have been elusive for some time now. The birds chirped as she passed by and many avid dog walkers enjoyed the frolicking of their favorite companion in this wondrous haven. Everyone acknowledged each other's presence with a smile, a pleasure derived from this mutual connection with nature and each other. Memories of yesterday no longer seemed so far away and were recaptured in that treasured moment of grace, with a clarity that could dazzle the heart and illuminate the mind.

The waves furled along the shoreline and the salty water kissed her cheeks. The sun was setting, with the colours flowing seamlessly in and out of the clouds. Young lovers stood barefoot at the edge of the pier holding hands and admiring the view. Jazz music from a nearby chalet wafted through the air, as a slight chill from the evening's gentle breeze made her skin prickle. Memories from the last few hours brought a smile to her lips as her mind assimilated every word and every nuance. Spirit understood this new beginning, and the start of a manifestation that she envisioned. Waiting had not been in vain and patience had drawn her closer to a triumphant success. The warmth in her eyes mirrored the luminous winks from the stars above, as love nestled comfortably in her heart. Her body swayed in rhythm with the music and the waves. As she fell under their spell, an unwavering peace grew within.

She danced through a garden of dreams in a field of marigolds, with keynotes of love upon her tongue. The trees swayed in the summer's breeze as the branches reached for one another in love. The colours of the sky were magnified by the bright smile of the sun. Her heart savoured this glorious moment, a present she knew was bestowed on everyone. Appreciating Mother Nature's beauty was one of the most precious gifts of affection offered by Heaven's love.

#6 - Dancing with Life

As we partner in this beautiful dance with Life, we recognize that what we see in others is also a very real part of ourselves, although at times we may act or feel separate. What we bring forth is quite significant. It includes our inner gifts, insightful nuggets of brilliance and our heart's glow. We have a great opportunity to choose how we want to participate in this wonderful…**Dance!**

Personal Mantra:

I choose to connect with my inner gifts and find creative ways of sharing them with others.

Personal Reflection:

What inspires you to create and play?

_____
_____
_____
_____
_____
_____
_____
_____
_____
_____

Kernels for Growth – Sprinkle with Love

Power Word:

Learning

> **"What we focus on can greatly enhance
> the quality of our LEARNING experience."**

#7 - Bold Celebration

Your heart is precious, and it is sacred. Everything you feel deeply touches a chord inside of you. There is great wisdom to be earned and understood in being able to bear witness to your heart's emotions. Celebrate all of your feelings as they are rewarding you in being your best...**Companion!**

Personal Mantra:

The more I open my heart, the more love flows through me.

Personal Reflection:

How do you manage or deal with emotions that make you feel uncomfortable?

_____
_____
_____
_____
_____
_____
_____
_____
_____
_____
_____
_____

Kernels for Growth – Sprinkle with Love

Power Word:

Forgiveness

**"FORGIVENESS is a gift with wings;
it is an opportunity to rise and fly freely."**

#8 - True Surrender

When we believe that there is a force in the universe that is working in co-creation with our intentions and our beliefs, there is something transformative in the way our life unfolds. We not only trust in ourselves, but we also trust that there is a plan at work designed for our highest…**Good!**

Personal Mantra:

I reach for ideas and plug into beliefs that support the grandest vision of my life.

Personal Reflection:

What are the beliefs that influence you the most while you are working towards the manifestation of your desires?

_____
_____
_____
_____
_____
_____
_____
_____
_____
_____

Kernels for Growth – Sprinkle with Love

Power Word:

Transformation

> **"TRANSFORMATION happens gradually; however, you may feel subtle shifts."**

_____
_____
_____
_____
_____
_____
_____
_____
_____
_____
_____
_____
_____
_____
_____
_____
_____
_____
_____
_____

Nathalie M. Léger

#9 - Communicating with Love

The use of words can be therapeutic, comforting and inviting. The way we use words can have a big impact on how we are communicating with others and how we are received. Language can make a world of difference when expressed and laced with good…**Intentions!**

Personal Mantra:

I am in tune with the expressions of love that seek to be communicated and bring value to my conversations with others.

Personal Reflection:

How do you use words to express your thoughts and emotions, and what impact do they have?

_____
_____
_____
_____
_____
_____
_____
_____
_____
_____
_____

Kernels for Growth – Sprinkle with Love

Power Word:

Self-expression

> **"When you are in the flow,
> you tap into your own form of SELF-EXPRESSION."**

#10 - Seeking Adventure

Adventure does not have to be thrill-seeking; it can be soul soothing. Sometimes the best cure for healing an overactive mind is retreating in nature, being immersed in the forest, going on a beautiful hike, or enjoying a moonlight stroll under the…**Stars!**

Personal Mantra:

I find myself among the trees and the mountains and I feel rejuvenated.

Personal Reflection:

What is one activity that you love, where you completely lose track of time?

_____

_____

_____

_____

_____

_____

_____

_____

_____

_____

_____

Power Word:

Connection

"A genuine CONNECTION is one that is unforgettable."

Nathalie M. Léger

Imagination

Travelling through flights of fancy
she can circle the world and witness
every waking possibility.

She knows that her innate
curiosity and the depths of
her questions are what gift her
with the most influential treasures
amid events that offer
prosperous adventures.

Dreams in Flight

You circled the globe reaping the rewards
of your own magnetized field.
Little by little you could feel the pulse
and the warmth emanating from sheer passion.
The timing of a perfect moment,
a burst of creative flames with an offer
and a map to the dream of a lifetime.

You had been groomed by the stirrings in your soul.
The guidance you carried within
became your instructor, sharing a flight plan
for your delightful departure into the exploration
of your open and vulnerable heart.

The excitement was palpable,
no turning back, only moving forward.
There was something altruistic about this proposal.
It was not tied to any attachment or expectations
that would yield unmet revelations.
It was a raw deal filled with
nuances and fruitful new beginnings,
a language of the heart…unfiltered.

A love so grand, a testament of living life
and merging with union of the highest calibre,
revered in appreciation and moments of
unequivocal power and feeling. A love so deep and true
shared and filled with memories of honest intentions come true.

Nathalie M. Léger

Soulful Imagery – In Awe of the Moment

There is this undeniable beauty that can be found in every breath. The eyes can only see a fraction of what the heart can detect. When open and receptive to the true nature of each moment, there is a pause where one can marvel still, dazzled by the revelation that seeks to appear through every waking experience in life.

Beauty emerges from the freedom to create without restrictions. It is the absolute surrender and the most innovative elixir for the heart. When you give yourself to the flow of inspiration emerging from self, therein lies the splendour and the soul of art.

We are made of sunlight and moonbeams. We are a delicate balance of both light and dark edges. Our beautifying emergence into light is meant to befriend our shadow and not discard it as if it was our enemy. When we become friends with our duality, the unification of these contrasting energies is what makes us whole.

The willow tree bows to the earth in gratitude for the stability it provides as its roots grow deep and it is filled with life. The seashells meld with the sands of time to be discovered by nature lovers who walk the beach in search of meaning and appreciation of simple moments. The earth offers us infinite ways in which our hearts can rejoice in the simplicity and grace of everyday living.

There is a richness that emanates from a life where guidance from the soul is honoured. These individuals are constantly sowing seeds of gratitude and sprinkling them with love. They cherish the path they have chosen. There is an enigmatic light that radiates from their being because they value the journey. There is a joyfulness and excitement that dances throughout their day. The passions that fire them up are the signs that are guiding them towards the fulfillment of their wishes. When one is in alignment with the treasures that are found within, when one listens to that inner voice that speaks in the stillness, when one moves with the flow of their life, they are relishing in all the wonders that are showered along the way.

Kernels for Growth – Sprinkle with Love

The tree is grieving, shedding old leaves, and burying a past in which a new autumn unearths forgiveness. A blanket of white covers the landscape, breathing new life to a winter of gifts delivering miracles. The beauty of the day springs from appreciation, marvelling from the love it feels in witnessing a flowering meadow. Sunny days warm our hearts, grassy meadows dress in green as honeybees dance in pairs with a sweet reminder to embrace the sweet nectar in our lives.

#11 – Aware in Wonder

We all have moments in our lives where everything seems to be in perfect alignment. It feels like luck and everything just seems to connect. Those perfect clicks can be inspiring, inviting you to look deeper into a situation and supporting you on your…**Path!**

Personal Mantra:

I feel that I am on my path and love is guiding me every step of the way forward.

Personal Reflection:

How does it make you feel to know that you are never alone in this world?

_____
_____
_____
_____
_____
_____
_____
_____
_____
_____
_____

Kernels for Growth – Sprinkle with Love

Power Word:

Blessings

> **"BLESSINGS feel like warm hugs wrapped in unconditional love."**

_____
_____
_____
_____
_____
_____
_____
_____
_____
_____
_____
_____
_____
_____
_____
_____
_____
_____
_____
_____

#12 – Simplicity of the Moment

There are times when life seems much more complex than it needs to be. In those moments where you feel your patience wearing thin, remember to take a deep breath. Sometimes that is all it takes when your mind is frazzled, and you are losing perspective. One simple…**Breath!**

Personal Mantra:

I concentrate on my breathing in those moments when I feel annoyed.

Personal Reflection:

What is the first thing you do when you are feeling stressed?

_____

_____

_____

_____

_____

_____

_____

_____

_____

_____

_____

Kernels for Growth – Sprinkle with Love

Power Word:

Strength

> **"Sometimes your STRENGTH is demonstrated by simply remaining silent."**

#13 – Fear Less

When you start understanding yourself more, you start to unravel every daunting fear that others will misunderstand you, and you simply become your vulnerable, amazing, and beautiful self. Now that is a mountain you want to climb because the view from the top will be… **Incredible!**

Personal Mantra:

I am discovering the seeds to my inner landscape that are welcoming me to flourish and shine.

Personal Reflection:

What is one realization you have uncovered about yourself and how has that changed your life?

_____
_____
_____
_____
_____
_____
_____
_____
_____
_____

Power Word:

Courage

> **"You act with COURAGE every time you disengage from a disempowering belief."**

#14 – Inclusive Collaboration

There is value in collaborating with others, whether it be helping each other out, combining talents, or engaging in exchanges that uplift, inspire and benefit two or more people. Life is good and can be even better when…**Sharing!**

Personal Mantra:

I find the nourishment I need by engaging with others and sharing my inspiration.

Personal Reflection:

What is one positive personal experience you have had when working with others?

_____
_____
_____
_____
_____
_____
_____
_____
_____
_____

Kernels for Growth – Sprinkle with Love

Power Word:

Experience

> **"EXPERIENCE is the souvenir of every *try* you've ever initiated."**

#15 – Act of Love

The more attuned you are to giving yourself love, the more love you can genuinely give and reciprocate to others. Love is more than a beautiful 4-letter word. It is an action that leaves a lingering essence of kindness and appreciation with those that you care to… **Love!**

Personal Mantra:

I know how love feels every time I connect to my own inner light.

Personal Reflection:

How do you show love to yourself in those moments when you feel disturbed by the unpredictability of life?

_____

_____

_____

_____

_____

_____

_____

_____

_____

_____

_____

Kernels for Growth – Sprinkle with Love

Power Word:

Integrity

**"You act from a place of INTEGRITY
when you honour and speak your truth."**

Nathalie M. Léger

In Sync

I dust off the last seeds of insight
that are hanging out
like cobwebs in my mind.

I revisit every thread
and I invite them
to flourish into this incredible story,
a narration of a fanciful
web of synchronicity
that connects this magical highway
with the crossroads in my life.

I indulge in the peculiarities
and the enchantment
I reap from noticing
the details that blend
so perfectly together.

I am in awe of the beauty
that emerges from the awareness
that is ever present in my day to day.

I am thankful for this gift.

Magic of the Heart

You may not always
understand the voice
of your soul.

It may be
contradictory
to the narrative
in your mind.

If you give
yourself enough
time to dive
deeper into the
well of your
own innate wisdom,

You will find
that the results
of exploring
feelings, rising
from deep within,
will always bestow
into your life
a series of
small delightful
miracles.

Nathalie M. Léger

Soulful Imagery – Everyday Magic

Everyday magic is the perfection in every moment and how Divine Intelligence is working through us for the manifestation of all that is. Everyone is free to choose what to believe. Some believe in the randomness of life and some believe in the mystical happenstance of life. There is no right or wrong choice in what to believe, but the results differ depending on which side we tend to lean towards.

I believe in the mystery of life and everyday serendipity. This kind of fascination fuels my creativity, and it brings a sense of aliveness and adventure that explores beyond the usual. When we open ourselves to what lies beyond the span of our five senses, we dive into worlds and worlds of information that have endless possibilities and can take us beyond anything we might have imagined.

I discover a world beyond the one we know and hear about. I am curious and I am moved by the unknown, the peculiar, and the in-betweens. I love to imagine and dream of things we cannot yet see. When we seek, we do find and in those moments of quiet revelation, the reality we thought we knew can be transformed before our very eyes.

There is a voice without words. Its intelligence rises from beneath layers and layers of stillness. When we escape the endless chatter in our mind, we can merge with this vastness, which plunges us into silence. It is within those depths that we can uncover the most profound elixir…the unequivocal splendour of absolute peace.

The leaves blushed in shades of autumn and the days grew darker and cooler. The house creaked as the wind sung tales of a past summer and the windows left traces of an evening frost glittering in morning's light. The streets were quiet and the living room's warmth from the fiery glow of flames rising in the fireplace generated such comfort and peace. The delectable aroma of warm bread and the lingering scent of blueberry tea was delightful. Slept-in sheets stayed rumpled at the foot of the bed as clothes were scattered all over the bedroom floor. The sound of running water could be heard from the bathroom and the soft melodic voice of an angel coming through the radio. Books were peeking from many different places as scribbled notes and pages of poetry were folded upon the desk in the study. Although it was quiet outside, there was this whole life happening inside. It was a precious one, a cherished gift, even though no one else was there to see it but her. She felt it from the moment she rose every morning. A prayer of gratitude and excitement for the blessings of this new day that was beginning. An adventure in the great art of what comes next. This grace, this joy, awakened from the call of her spirit. A life she chose from the passion in her veins, the love in her heart and the one that made her whole being smile.

#16 – Inner Beauty

Inner beauty translates into outer beauty as it emanates from the purity of your heart. It is a radiance that comes from authenticity and valuing confidence. When you tap into your well of appreciation for life, you bring light to everything that you…**Do!**

Personal Mantra:

When I value myself and share from a place of self-worth, I find myself glowing from the inside out.

Personal Reflection:

What does confidence feel and look like to you?

_____
_____
_____
_____
_____
_____
_____
_____
_____
_____
_____
_____

Kernels for Growth – Sprinkle with Love

Power Word:

Radiance

**"Your RADIANCE is magnetic
and can create an everlasting impression."**

#17 – Purposeful Goodness

Your purpose lies in the details of your life. It does not have to be LOUD and BIG. It can be SIMPLE and QUIET. You know you are living your purpose by how it feels. Are you happy with the life you are living? Does your life bring meaning to the lives of others? If so, you are on the path...**Smile**!

Personal Mantra:

I am living my inner truth and it guides me towards bringing a wealth of genuine offerings to others.

Personal Reflection:

What is one thing that you do consistently that makes you feel good?

_____

_____

_____

_____

_____

_____

_____

_____

_____

_____

_____

Power Word:

Valuable

> **"Your time and your energy are your most VALUABLE assets and investments."**

#18 – Making Time

Make it a priority every day to welcome time for yourself. It is important to know when enough is enough and it is time to rest. Your body knows it and will give you subtle signs at first. Learn to recognize these signs and act on them before they become much bigger to deal with. You are…**Important!**

Personal Mantra:

I know that when I am tired and confused, I need to make time to refuel and re-energize.

Personal Reflection:

How do you know when you need to retreat and take a break?

_____
_____
_____
_____
_____
_____
_____
_____
_____
_____
_____

Kernels for Growth – Sprinkle with Love

Power Word:

Introspection

**"INTROSPECTION stretches the mind;
the deeper you go, the more pliable it becomes"**

#19 – Romance is in the Air

What does romance look like? It may not be experienced in the same way for everyone. For some, it may look like a box of chocolates or flowers, while for others it may be taking a walk under the stars or sitting by a campfire holding hands. It may even look like your significant other wearing an apron and making your favourite meal. Everyone has their idea of a romantic getaway, but one thing is for sure, when true romance is in the air, you feel…**It!**

Personal Mantra:

I enjoy experiences where romance flourishes organically, since it makes the experiences even more memorable.

Personal Reflection:

What is your ideal romantic setting?

_____

_____

_____

_____

_____

_____

_____

_____

_____

Kernels for Growth – Sprinkle with Love

Power Word:

Sensuality

**"SENSUALITY is an invitation
to connect with all of your senses."**

#20 – Developing Intuition

Intuition is a safeguard that gives you access to your own personal wisdom and guides you towards clarity and truth. Intuition is your most trusted friend and counsellor. To understand how your intuition works takes practice, and the curiosity to...**Explore!**

Personal Mantra:

I am on a journey of discovery to explore the subtle differences between my intuition and wishful thinking.

Personal Reflection:

Can you recall a time when your intuition was encouraging you to take that leap of faith?

_____
_____
_____
_____
_____
_____
_____
_____
_____
_____
_____
_____

Kernels for Growth – Sprinkle with Love

Power Word:

Curiosity

> **"CURIOSITY leads to adventure and astounding discoveries."**

Nathalie M. Léger

Timing of a Moment

I remember the weeping willow's
shine in the moonlight that night,
how radiant it glowed
even though its branches
were showing signs of melancholy.

I remember the echo of the wind
moving through the air, a soft
breeze, barely audible,
but felt at a palpable level
of shimmering hope.

I remember the look you wore,
the depth of your longing
unveiling your love, in harmony
with that perfect time,
one you had patiently waited for.

I remember that magical
feeling, being swept in
the enchantment of the moment;
the embodiment of a dream
awakening to its life.

If You Know Love, Then You Do...

Love is in the doing and the unravelling.
It is found in the quiet moments and the undercurrents
between breath and sound.

It is a mixture of joy and tears,
so sublime that even the sunset can get jealous of
its exquisite display of colours.

It is a dance between tenderness and passion,
a connection from soul to heart.
It is found in the peaks and valleys,
unearthing stirring passions and reverberating belly laughs.

There is a mirror at play,
unmasking pretense and inspiring vulnerability,
murmuring promises under shaded trees
and stealing auspicious kisses under
the shine of a glowing moon.

Nathalie M. Léger

Soulful Imagery – Divine Feminine

She knows how to entertain both her darkness and her light. She is not afraid to step into the shaded alleys of her soul and work through the cobwebs of discovery. She also knows how to honour her light and does not dim it for fear of it glowing too brightly.

The Divine Feminine is moved by the flow of her innate creativity. She is always in the process of transformation. Her joy is found through her profound awareness and understanding that everything in nature is in flux, and through this unfolding, the opportunity to flourish is presented in perfect time and divine rhythm. She recognizes that there is a strength within a woman that is unbound when she learns to stand humbled by her own light and withdraws from standing as a mere shadow of others. She is learning to embrace this beautiful gift with modesty and grace.

She loves to dance with flowers in her hair, seduced by the sultry midnight stars hanging in a distant universe. She reaches high and pulls each one close, whispering secrets, wishes that have been nesting in her heart. She gifts them back to the beautiful night sky as she blows a kiss to the moon smiling from above. She makes love to the earth, feet cushioned on a blanket of grass as the sound of a waterfall sings her a lullaby. She stands contentedly admiring the flames of the campfire as she enjoys the gentle caress of the wind enveloping her in blanket of love.

She has met the empress within and has created chapter upon chapter from the wisdom and lessons learned. She has emerged as the leading lady in the movie of her life, the one she was destined to be. Every experience and love entertained rests in the memory of her heart, which is full of joy and everlasting light.

Kernels for Growth – Sprinkle with Love

>I am free, I choose to be;
>I am goddess, I create with heart;
>I am empress, I draw from soul;
>I am flow; I lose my mind.

I ride the waves, navigating through the waters of my heart. I tend to my garden, planting seeds in the earth under my feet. I ignite with light as I tune in to the fire in my belly. I listen, still, breathing in the air swirling with love.

Nathalie M. Léger

#21 – Silent Vows

There is an inner sanctuary where you can retreat whenever you want. It is the place within, where you meet with your inner guru and merge with your inner light. You find peace and harmony in this space and it is…**Priceless!**

Personal Mantra:

When I move into this space of pure light, I delve into a transformative experience that leaves me feeling peaceful and loved.

Personal Reflection:

Do you have a song, a meditation practice or a hobby that makes you feel completely at peace?

_____

_____

_____

_____

_____

_____

_____

_____

_____

_____

_____

Kernels for Growth – Sprinkle with Love

Power Word

Invitation

**"An INVITATION from your soul
is gifting you a memorable experience."**

#22 – Earnest Accountability

A life with purpose honours accountability. When you can sit with yourself in complete honesty and be truly aware of what works in your life and what does not, you are in a position of immense authentic power. You are truly in the driver's seat of your own... **Life!**

Personal Mantra:

I have tremendous potential for making amazing things happen in my life, and for which I am accountable, and respectfully so.

Personal Reflection:

How do you demonstrate to others that you are accountable for the choices that you make?

_____
_____
_____
_____
_____
_____
_____
_____
_____
_____
_____

Kernels for Growth – Sprinkle with Love

Power Word:

Acceptance

> **"ACCEPTANCE opens the door to newfound insights and light-filled revelations."**

_____
_____
_____
_____
_____
_____
_____
_____
_____
_____
_____
_____
_____
_____
_____
_____
_____
_____
_____
_____

#23 – Endless Generosity

The energy from giving generously from an open heart is immeasurable. It is a feeling that grows and grows the more we do it. There is a sentiment of irreplaceable grace in the act of giving from this fullness that flows with incessant…**Ease!**

Personal Mantra:

I find joy in giving, and the act of sharing without expectation attracts abundance in droves.

Personal Reflection:

What has been your greatest realization from giving without attachment to outcome?

_____
_____
_____
_____
_____
_____
_____
_____
_____
_____

Kernels for Growth – Sprinkle with Love

Power Word:

Creativity

> **"CREATIVITY is genuinely expressed through boundless flow."**

#24 – Honouring Creativity

You have a well of creativity that is unlimited and boundless. When you find within what makes you soar with enthusiasm, and play with wild abandon, you learn to paint your days in a medley of colours and find meaning in a variety of...**Ways!**

Personal Mantra:

I give myself to the inspiration that is calling out to me. "Come out to play; let us enjoy another day!"

Personal Reflection:

What is the most exciting creative project you have completed?

_____
_____
_____
_____
_____
_____
_____
_____
_____
_____
_____
_____

Kernels for Growth – Sprinkle with Love

Power Word:

Freedom

"FREEDOM is being able to colour outside the lines."

_____
_____
_____
_____
_____
_____
_____
_____
_____
_____
_____
_____
_____
_____
_____
_____
_____
_____
_____
_____
_____
_____
_____

#25 – Joyful Introspection

We learn more and more about ourselves each day by being present to our thoughts and our emotions. Every time we catch ourselves reacting or feeling uneasy in a situation about something someone said or information that does not resonate, it is an opportunity to explore it even…**Deeper!**

Personal Mantra:

I am present to what is being activated within and pause to recognize the underlying message it is trying to bring to light.

Personal Reflection:

What is one recurring theme that seems to surface in conversations that incites strong emotions within you?

_____
_____
_____
_____
_____
_____
_____
_____
_____
_____

Power Word:

Listening

> **"Active LISTENING is both a practice and an art."**

Nathalie M. Léger

Inward Vows

A union of a
love so complete
first starts with
a vow you make
to yourself.

It is one you
revisit daily
and honour
with gratitude
and fidelity.

It is a love
so sacred that
no one should
ever come
between you
and your integrity.

Embrace your worth
and value the
preciousness that
you are.

As you do,
life will blossom
in this magnificent garden
and the stars will
be shining on you.

Mirror of Enchantment

The string of pearls
sat at the foot of the bed
while she brushed out
her long locks of
brown hair.

A smile twinkled
in her eyes as she
looked in the mirror
and visions of his
lingering kiss on her
shoulder danced
through
her mind.

The burst of light
from the silhouette
of the moon shone
through the window,
amidst a warm glow
of romance and candlelight.

A night of dreams,
manifestations of
ethereal wishes and
dreams in flight
grew with new breaths
and cascading waves of
love coming to life.

Nathalie M. Léger

Soulful Imagery – A New Dawn

Can you still feel the everlasting traces of my love and the presence offered from my open heart, a complete manifestation of my sincerity and devotion to you?

She could feel the warmth and the energy of Heaven's light bathing her in a blanket of sparkling diamonds. She could feel the joy and the pleasure of universal playfulness arousing her creativity in a medley of new ideas and daydreams.

Stepping into her power and gripped by the sheer intensity of her own love, she meets her strength and merges with the infinite faith harbouring within. With each breath of life, she is touched by the hand of humility and finds her perfect mirror in the benevolence of the Universe.

She knows that the eyes of wisdom lie within the landscape of her own intrinsic nature, an intelligence which makes her life spark with aliveness and light up with meaning. There is nowhere to go but within; everything that can be appreciated on the outside first needs to be acknowledged from the inside.

A heart that constantly believes waters the seeds of wisdom that it garners along the way. It sprinkles them faithfully with care and inspiration. A heart that believes is grateful for its crops of forgiveness and compassion that help it journey forward when it feels disheartened or imprisoned. A heart that believes knows it is never alone in this world. On the path, it is reminded of Heaven's love through memory and intuition, and can feel the energetic presence and light shining from the angels above.

Kernels for Growth – Sprinkle with Love

A brush of her lips can speak
the words so needed to heal
a heart that is longing
to be loved and heard.

The simple touch of her hand
can caress and temper a mind
full of worry and strife.

There is magic in her eyes and compassion in her heart.

#26 – Enabling Truth

Your truth invites you on a journey and when you follow your heart, you meet yourself. It is through this invitation from "Self" that you start witnessing your life through the eyes of alignment. You begin to live with more authenticity and…**Integrity!**

Personal Mantra:

I am discovering my inner truths, which are welcoming the birth of new ideas and following the stream of my vital purpose.

Personal Reflection:

What truth about yourself makes you feel most alive and free?

_____

_____

_____

_____

_____

_____

_____

_____

_____

_____

_____

Kernels for Growth – Sprinkle with Love

Power Word:

Harmony

"HARMONY offers relief to a restless mind."

#27 – Leading with Courage

When you fear rejection, act with courage; otherwise, you will be denying yourself the perfection of that moment. Sometimes, the things that you are meant to do, and which are part of your life plan, will be mixed in with a bit of apprehension as they appear. Do not let that dissuade you. Be bold in the pursuit of your…**Happiness!**

Personal Mantra:

I am venturing into the unknown, yet I trust that I will learn from new experiences that are meant to offer me new knowledge and wisdom.

Personal Reflection:

Can you recall an opportunity that made you nervous, even though you still went ahead with it and shone?

_____
_____
_____
_____
_____
_____
_____
_____
_____
_____

Kernels for Growth – Sprinkle with Love

Power Word:

Imagination

"Your IMAGINATION is like an adventure park, the ultimate playground in your mind."

#28 – Success in Layers

Self-worth, self-acceptance, self-care, self-love, and self-validation all have one common denominator: they all start with yourself. If you do not know how to fill your cup, no one else will, or will ever be able to keep it filled. Personal success begins and ends with you. You have every reason to celebrate your own…**Worth!**

Personal Mantra:

I am confident in the pursuit of success, as I feel worthy of abundance and great love.

Personal Reflection:

What does personal success mean to you?

_____
_____
_____
_____
_____
_____
_____
_____
_____
_____
_____

Kernels for Growth – Sprinkle with Love

Power Word:

Balance

> **"The perfect BALANCE exists in your daily life;
> you just have to find the key."**

#29 – Finding Peace

When you face unpredictability or you are experiencing moments that are stressful, those are perfect opportunities for you to practice self-awareness. Once you identify what you are feeling, you are in a better position to react in a different way. Please remember that you can always go within and choose…**Peace!**

Personal Mantra:

I find peace in moments of stillness, and find myself falling deeper and deeper in love with silence.

Personal Reflection:

Is there a specific environment or setting that helps you unwind?

_____
_____
_____
_____
_____
_____
_____
_____
_____
_____
_____

Kernels for Growth – Sprinkle with Love

Power Word:

Laughter

> **"Every bout of LAUGHTER can succeed in generating a rainfall of happy tears."**

#30 – Desire to Prosper

When you acknowledge your great responsibility in this world and your desire to find the light that guides your way, you are already set on a course of positivity in a great state of flow filled with thriving... **Adventure!**

Personal Mantra:

I am here, fully present, and I desire nothing less than to fully flourish from this light emitting from my being.

Personal reflection:

What do you envision that you need to succeed?

_____
_____
_____
_____
_____
_____
_____
_____
_____
_____
_____
_____

Kernels for Growth – Sprinkle with Love

Power Word:

Abundance

> **"ABUNDANCE is a growth mindset;
> what you believe amplifies."**

Nathalie M. Léger

Rewarding Pause

She bathed in a pool
of shimmering light
and frolicked in
laughter, enjoying
a slothful day which
presented an opportunity
for unhurried action
and lounging pleasure.

She relaxed into
the stillness, taking
pause to relish
the moment,
like a luxurious massage
that invited her body and
mind to rest in lavish
abundance and ever
present peace.

On a Journey to Love

As I sit here
and pen
the memories
of my past

I embrace and value
the importance
of every experience.

I find comfort
in the memories,
I find humour
in the follies,
I find innocence
through the eyes
of curiosity.

In my desire for growth,
every avenue and every
path has brought me
to this moment.

I am standing still
and remembering life,
one filled with
joy and loyalty,
courage and respect,
on a journey to love.

Nathalie M. Léger

Soulful Imagery – A Lover's Journey

Life's boldest adventure begins with the brilliance of this one simple realization.

"True love" begins in the abyss of each heart, and from this genuine illumination, all other loves thereafter are transformed by the alchemy of one's inner lighthouse.

A lover's journey is a sacred commitment to a path, which is expressed through the unfolding of dreams incarnated from the flames of unquenchable passion, a desire to create what is sincere and true in affirmation to one's own purpose and destiny. Every step towards the manifestation of artful creation stems from an undying love affair with imagination. When the inner lover awakens, every state of its evolution bestows new gifts to appreciate.

The alchemy starts to occur as a person shifts into the awareness stage of questioning. A quest is now underway, and the veil slowly begins to lift. Little by little, new truths begin to form as one discovers their true nature. Everything that may have appeared real starts to unravel and is revealed to be illusion.

A moment of illumination feels like when you look up and see the dark sky blanketed with stars. It is that precise moment when every twinkle of light forms a web of brilliance and you are moved by the sheer perfection of its harmonious design.

A lover's heart holds nothing back. It is vulnerable and does not lack initiative. It is fully open and paves the way to its soul lit destination. It does not renounce the opportunities to learn; it celebrates the occasions offering expansion and marvels in the love and beauty of its lifelong journey.

The lover surrenders and watches as time slips through the eye of the needle, a fine thread of golden sand stitched on the wings of eternity. Time remembers to bare old beliefs and becomes the witness to the remembrance of unconditional love; it marvels at all that moves us towards greater compassion, the synchronistic magic that weaves in out and out of our lives, leaving glitters of hope on the majestic canvas of humanity.

Inner guidance is just one of the many beautiful gifts each lover's heart is born with. When in touch with its essence, the lover's heart moves into the flow of its life and rejoices in celebration. Its energy is just so vibrant that it enlivens all of the senses. It sees and envisions a world filled with light and abundance for all. The lover's transformation is essential and an embodiment of the beauty that lives at the core of every human being.

Epilogue

> With every breath
> You go deeper,
> With every step
> You move closer,
> With every wish
> You shine brighter.

I named this poem **In the Flow.** This book is a manifestation of being in a state of flow. When you are in the flow, everything is possible. I want to thank you for joining me on this journey. I hope that you enjoyed the journaling exercises and will benefit from my kernels for growth and be inspired to find your own. Life is continually inviting us to grow and prosper.

We are surrounded by so many beautiful reasons to follow our hearts and live out our most precious daydreams. When you are excited about exploring something, listen well and give yourself permission to go within and connect to what speaks to you. Remain curious and discover your original blend of creativity. Dabble with different ideas and act on some of the thoughts that seem to pop up, out of the blue. Sometimes, a single thought can have a domino effect and lead you towards something phenomenal. The way you live your life becomes a testament of who you are. You have a purpose. Isn't that something pretty amazing to contemplate? There is no one exactly like you and that is your incredible gift to the world.

We have endless opportunities to meet numerous people on our journey. Many of them become incredibly special and some may even become some of our most influential companions. I believe that everyone we meet has such an important purpose to fulfill in our lives, as we do in theirs. Every encounter, no matter how brief, has the potential to offer us a gift. It is not the length of time we spend with someone that is important. It is the quality of the experience we have with that person that becomes significant. There is nothing more exquisite than being in the presence of someone who is unapologetically radiating with joy and living a life of unabashed purpose. Step into your light and shine, you are worth it!

I am so grateful to everyone I have met on my own journey; I am filled with immense appreciation. I have benefited from the kernels they have brought into my life, from the smallest lesson learned, to all the memories that still live on long after they have been shared. I have gained from every love that has captured my heart, every opportunity that has invited me to share my abundant enthusiasm, my passion for life, every creative desire that has moved me to share from a place of love. Thank you to everyone I am honoured to celebrate the rest of this great life with. May we share and enjoy many countless hours in deep conversation, play, laughter, love, and unlimited creativity.

May all your **Kernels for Growth** flourish in a series of captivating and heart riveting wonders!

Nathalie M. Léger

Your Journal

Journaling is a great way to start your day or a wonderful way to relax before bedtime. These extra pages are meant to be filled with the precious time you spend, connecting with your…**Heart!**

_____
_____
_____
_____
_____
_____
_____
_____
_____
_____
_____
_____
_____
_____
_____
_____
_____
_____
_____

Kernels for Growth – Sprinkle with Love

Nathalie M. Léger

Kernels for Growth – Sprinkle with Love

Nathalie M. Léger

Kernels for Growth – Sprinkle with Love

Nathalie M. Léger

Kernels for Growth – Sprinkle with Love

Nathalie M. Léger

Kernels for Growth – Sprinkle with Love

Nathalie M. Léger

Kernels for Growth – Sprinkle with Love

Nathalie M. Léger

Kernels for Growth – Sprinkle with Love

Nathalie M. Léger